SPOTLIGHT ON
AN EQUITABLE WORLD

CREATING SOLUTIONS

Mary Ratzer

ROSEN
PUBLISHING

Published in 2025 by The Rosen Publishing Group, Inc.
2544 Clinton Street, Buffalo, NY 14224

First Edition

Editor: Greg Roza
Book Design: Michael Flynn

Photo Credits: Cover Ground Picture/Shutterstock.com; cover, p. 3 (hands) Dedraw Studio/Shutterstock.com; (series Earth icon) v4ndhira/Shutterstock.com; p. 5 Nancy Kaszerman/ZUMA Press/Alamy; p. 6 Photoroyalty/Shutterstock.com; p. 7 Prostock-studio/Shutterstock.com; p. 8 PeopleImages.com - Yuri A/Shutterstock.com; p. 9 1000 Words/Shutterstock.com; p. 11 vk_st/Shutterstock.com; pp. 13, 17 CREATISTA/Shutterstock.com; p. 14 YES Market Media/Shutterstock.com; p. 15 https://commons.wikimedia.org/wiki/File:FEMA_-_7978209.jpg; p. 18 mooremedia/Shutterstock.com; p. 19 p_ponomareva/Shutterstock.com; p. 21 Monkey Business Images/Shutterstock.com; p. 22 airdone/Shutterstock.com; p. 23 https://commons.wikimedia.org/wiki/File:MalalaYousafzai_-_13008047475.jpg; p. 25 BAZA Production/Shutterstock.com; p. 26 paulaphoto/Shutterstock.com; p. 27 AlessandroBiascioli/Shutterstock.com; p. 29 https://commons.wikimedia.org/wiki/File:South_Philadelphia_High_School_2101_S_Broad_St_Philadelphia_PA_(DSC_2838).jpg/Shutterstock.com.

Library of Congress Cataloging-in-Publication Data

Names: Ratzer, Mary Boyd, author.
Title: Creating solutions / Mary Ratzer.
Description: [Buffalo] : Rosen Publishing, [2025] | Series: Spotlight on an equitable world | Includes index.
Identifiers: LCCN 2023055853 (print) | LCCN 2023055854 (ebook) | ISBN 9781499477221 (library binding) | ISBN 9781499477337 (paperback) | ISBN 9781499476941 (ebook)
Subjects: LCSH: Social problems--Juvenile literature. | Social change--Juvenile literature. | Problem solving--Juvenile literature. | Communities--Juvenile literature. | Community development--Juvenile literature.
Classification: LCC HN18.3 .R37 2025 (print) | LCC HN18.3 (ebook) | DDC 361.2--dc23/eng/20231220
LC record available at https://lccn.loc.gov/2023055853
LC ebook record available at https://lccn.loc.gov/2023055854

Manufactured in the United States of America

CPSIA Compliance Information: Batch #CSRYA25. For further information contact Rosen Publishing at 1-800-237-9932.

CONTENTS

Chapter One

PUTTING IT ALL TOGETHER

Look around: creative solutions for problems are happening in communities right now! Just look at and listen to the real world. Big and small, creative solutions take shape. Creative solutions entail a problem, caring members of a community, resources, creative solutions, partnerships, and action.

Look at the fire that destroyed the town of Lahaina on the Hawaiian island of Maui in the summer of 2023. Winds up to 80 miles (128 km) per hour swept a massive fire over an entire community, destroying 2,200 homes. This fire's destructive force cost many lives and everything the people there owned. When the fire ended, most of the town was gone.

Everyone in Lahaina needed help. Active citizens took on one immediate and desperate need. How could the victims of this fire get food and water? How could caring citizens solve this almost impossible problem? Caring people with expert knowledge and volunteers with skills came together in response.

The owner and head chef of a restaurant that was destroyed decided to produce enough meals to feed her island. Lee Ann Wong, a master chef, tapped a nearby university cooking school and its huge kitchen. She found partners in teachers at the school and other island chefs. Her team prepared and shared 6,000 meals a day! Volunteers transported them to shelters and handed them out to the hungry. Chef Alex Gleason prepared over 5,000 meals a day in his restaurant that survived the fires. Chefs all over Hawaii cooked, packaged, transported, and shared food for the people of Lahaina. This is what a creative solution looks like!

In an interview soon after the fire destroyed her restaurant, Wong (shown here) said, "I didn't really have time to stop and take a beat . . . . Our community mobilized right away."

Chapter Two

CREATIVITY

Creative thinking is at the heart of finding solutions for problems. Using creativity, you can find a way to produce an original idea, plan, design, or possibility. Creative people solve problems. They ask questions, explore, plan, invent, connect, and produce. Creativity is often fueled by collaboration and the energy of many minds. Sometimes one person shines through, such as Orlando.

This ninth grader, who lives in an urban community, suffered from a digestive disorder called celiac disease. Problems with digesting certain foods kept him from attending school many days. Truant officers knew him well. Orlando had an English teacher who challenged her class to a semester-long project called Create Change. Students decided on a project goal that was important to them. They

Do you have a message you want to share with the community? You could write and perform and song just like Orlando did!

had freedom to use class time for researching, producing creative work, and sharing. Their creative teacher provided encouragement.

Orlando started to show up and do work on his project. He wrote an original rap song dedicated to others with his health problem. He designed a website providing information and support for teens with celiac disease. It proudly featured his rap song and his creative message.

When complete, the website started getting thousands of hits. Orlando experienced the rewards of his own creative mind and empathy for others. Orlando kept coming to school and returned in grade 10 as a mentor to the new ninth graders as they launched their own Create Change project.

Chapter Three

PROBLEMS SOLVED

Look at creative solutions for problems affecting the needs and rights of others. Explore how this works and see the patterns. Can you add examples to the following problems and solutions that you see in your own real world?

Problem: Major League Baseball (MLB) has seen a drop in the number of Black athletes in the league. In the 1940s, Black baseball players broke the race barrier and for many decades have been an important part of the sport. But since the 1990s, the percent of Black players in the league has steadily declined.
Solution: The MLB started a program to draw promising Black players into the sport. The athletes participate in camps with workouts, interviews, and games where they showcase their skills. In July 2023, one in six of the athletes at combine were talented Black players.

Airports are busy and noisy most of the day. People with sensory issues may have a hard time navigating the airport and locating their flight in time.

Problem: People with autism spectrum disorder are often more sensitive to stimulus in their surroundings than others are. Busy places with a lot of lights and noises can be challenging locations for a growing number of young people. Airports, libraries, stores, athletic events, and a variety of other experiences can create stress for those with sensory issues.

Solutions: A business can meet the needs of these customers by hosting a sensory-friendly hour. Sensory-friendly hours include reduced noise, lighting, and crowds. Sensory rooms are a part of public places such as libraries and museums. Special hours are set aside for low-sensory experiences in hospitals. Airports offer special air travel opportunities where children are guided through what to expect while in the airport, boarding a plane, and flying.

Chapter Four

GETTING TO SOLUTIONS

Sergio Peralta was born with a birth defect—a hand that didn't fully form. When Peralta started a new school year at Hendersonville High School, he hid his hand, but a teacher in the engineering department found out. Students in an engineering class in Tennessee created a hand for a new student in their school!

Finding solutions involves creativity, people skills, teamwork, and a thorough understanding of the problem. The teacher's engineering students were willing to create a prosthetic hand with their knowledge using a 3D printer and online models. The project took the class four weeks designing and sizing a prototype hand. Sergio said the hand changed his life for the better.

Problem-solving has a beginning, a middle, and an end. In the beginning you define the problem. You analyze and investigate. Understanding the problem well is key to solving it. In the middle of the process, you work on brainstorming many ideas and then decide what would be the best action to take. With an idea for a solution, you look at what you need to make the idea work. The resources, people, and information needed to complete a project need to be identified. Once these steps are taken, a plan begins to take shape.

The next step is the action step. Teams or individuals accomplish what is needed for the planned solution. One last step is needed. You try out your solution and determine if it works. If you succeed, you have learned from your success. If you fail, reflect on the solution and evaluate your results. Then you can try another plan.

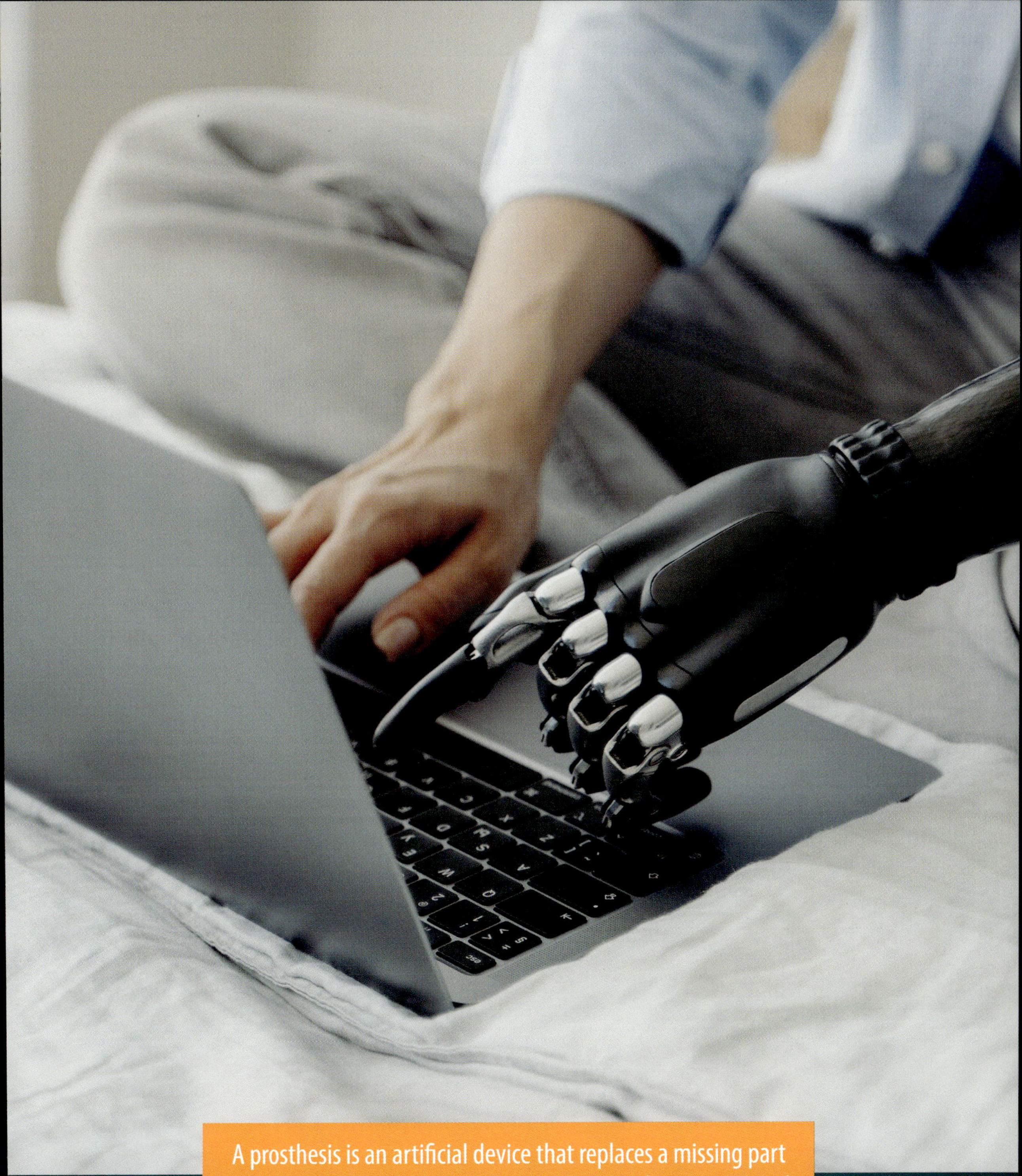

A prosthesis is an artificial device that replaces a missing part of the body. Modern prosthetics are capable of movement and can give disabled people a chance to do things others can do.

Chapter Five

TEEN MENTORS

A 12th-grade English teacher knew her final research paper assignment didn't mean much to her students. Completing it was an unwelcome task based on topics that had no connection to the learners' lives. She came up with a creative solution after an open discussion with her students about another approach to their senior project. Students agreed to journal for one week about what they observed in their real world that needed a creative solution. Sharing their journals, many personal and social issues came up.

The class decided to break up into teams and tackle solutions for problems they identified. One chose to look at drunk driving in their rural community. Another investigated the high drop-out rate by their peers attempting to transition to the regional community college after graduating from high school. A third team came up with a creative solution to help students transitioning from the middle school to the high school. This solution became part of that school's culture.

The third team interviewed middle school students about their fears, questions, and expectations. They shared what they had heard about high school and felt they weren't ready for the social and academic challenges. Investigating what other schools did to solve this problem, the team created a Teen Mentoring Project. The high school students adopted a middle schooler and mentored them in a Get Ready Camp during the summer. The team also recruited juniors to be ready to engage with middle schoolers earlier in the school year and support them in dealing with social and academic problems. This shows that peer-to-peer support makes a big difference.

Do you have any talents you could share with your peers? For example, if you like the theater and putting on plays you could join a local youth theater to share what you know.

Chapter Six

PITCHING IN

American values have often stressed self-reliance and individual independence. Ethics in competitive sports, business, and achieving success often focus on putting oneself first. However, many of the religions of the world encourage service to others balanced with your own needs. These religions emphasize compassion, being your brother's keeper, and kindness as the basis of just action. Many cultures within this country strongly value pitching in to help others.

Many hometown heroes do exactly that. Firefighters, members of the military, healthcare workers, and many others pitch in to make life better for everyone. These selfless people are routinely part of creative solutions for their communities. Valuing service to others means pitching in.

The Coral Springs, Florida, police department conducts the One Team—One Mission food distribution project. This project collects and provides food for those in need.

In August 2023, wildfires destroyed about 80 percent of the Hawaiian town of Lahaina on the island of Maui. In the true spirit of kokua, people from all over the world came to Lahaina to help the local people rebuild their community.

Disasters such as earthquakes and floods shine a light on how people depend on each other. No solutions are possible without the care and courage of strangers who pitch in. Those who pitch in often believe that their purpose is to help their community to thrive. In Hawaii, many live by the concept of *kokua*. Kokua means showing love and giving generous help to others for their benefit, not for personal gain. Many native Hawaiian people share their strengths and talents without expecting anything in return.

These values show themselves in your peer group, neighborhood, and larger community. Creative solutions work for human needs and a better community when people pitch in and work together. This is your time to decide on your values. This is your time to try being a caring citizen and see how it works for you.

Chapter Seven

WHAT IS THE BIG IDEA?

Starting with a goal in mind gives you a purpose for anything you do. Perhaps you could consider the goal of becoming an active citizen who works to solve problems in the community. How can you learn about creative solutions and taking civic action to solve problems for others? Educators, leaders, and involved members of the community can support young people in learning how to make a difference. Skills needed for civic action are an important topic for social studies learners in middle school and high school.

Countless young people connect with their communities and solve problems. They work with unique needs, resources, interests, and partners. Perhaps peers in your school are already a part of civic action. Creating solutions through civic action is just an idea until you decide to give it a try. Just being aware of problems is challenging. Moving your focus to the needs of others widens your perceptions. Your values and beliefs may motivate you to step up.

You can learn practical skills from extracurricular activities or service projects in school. Discussing current events and issues can inspire you to take action. Being a member of school committees or a club leader gives you practice with planning, decision-making, and personal responsibility. Working with a group such as the Scouts, 4H, a sports team, or getting a part-time job gives you experience with collaboration, relationships, communication, and even creativity. Your real world is a training ground.

The 4H Club has been functioning for over 100 years. It's a great place for teens to learn hands-on projects in health, science, agriculture, and civic engagement. Adult volunteers and mentors guide youth members and encourage them to take on leadership roles in the community.

Chapter Eight

WHO YOU ARE AND WHAT YOU DO

Problems are part of your real world. They impact people you know and people in your community. They can be important to you. Problems need problem solvers. As a young person who belongs to a community, your decisions and choices can make you part of creating solutions. Who you are motivates what you do.

The moment you decide to be part of solving a problem, you are choosing to be a caring and active citizen. You are choosing to recognize the problem and understand it. You are choosing to improve a situation and talk about it with your peers. You can analyze the causes and consequences of the problem. As a partner with others, you can explore your role as a caring citizen. Social responsibility leads you to work for the well-being of others. By engaging in advocacy and action, you work for your community.

It is fulfilling to help others in your community. You can share your skills and talents while making the community a better place to live!

How does this work in everyday experience? These traits are visible evidence of your identity and the person you are. They easily drive your choices, decisions, and your actions.

- **You are curious and open minded.**
- **You are honest and fair.**
- **You make judgments after analyzing information and facts.**
- **You identify solutions for personal and social problems.**
- **You understand and evaluate the consequences of your actions.**
- **You recognize the value of critical thinking skills both inside and outside of school.**
- **You reflect on your role to promote personal, family, and community well-being.**
- **You understand safety concerns for yourself and others.**

Chapter Nine

THE SELFIE VS. THE UNSELFIE

Dr. Michele Borba wrote a book called *The Unselfie: Why Empathetic Kids Succeed in Our All-About-Me World*. Borba has studied empathy for many years and uses the selfie photographs that flood social media to make her point.

Borba asserts there is a connection between the endless taking of selfie photos with smartphones and a sharp drop in empathy in middle grade and high school students. The taking and sharing of selfies is evidence of strong self-interest. This goes hand in hand with a drop in caring and empathetic behavior. Borba believes this trend needs to be recognized and reversed for many reasons.

For many teens, the shift away from in-person interaction can result in a drop in empathy for others. With the COVID-19 pandemic partly to blame, a significant amount of social interaction has moved to digital devices. For some, this has caused a drop in understanding of emotions and how they are communicated. Empathy depends on reading physical messages that tell how someone is feeling. Facetime or other digital tools fail to be a match for person-to-person sharing.

Empathetic kids have what has been called the "empathy advantage." Helping kids to understand others helps them to build healthy relationships. Kids who sense another person's emotions can ask questions and make better choices about how to react or how to help. Kids who understand the importance of empathy demonstrate that value in their actions when they help others. They are an asset to a group, a class, a school, and a community.

It's fun to share photographs of yourself on social media sites where your friends can view and comment on them. However, selfies are no replacement for in-person contact.

Chapter Ten

LEADING THE WAY

Leadership skills give young people the ability to make things happen. Practicing leadership skills gives teens confidence and helps them solve problems. Adults should support young leaders but should not take away control of decisions, projects, and planning. So often teens and middle schoolers use creativity to solve problems especially when they work together. Leaders work in a team, and work collaboratively with others. Their impact on the community as a team is far greater than any single person could accomplish. Young people develop responsibility and organization when they discover their leadership ability.

Often, young leaders can inspire others. Their energy and ideas for positive change connect with others involved in the effort. They can motivate others to use their talents and strengths for a positive goal. Being the leader only works when others engage with the effort you're making. Some adolescents just discover their ability to make a positive change happen. Clear communication with others and listening to ideas and knowledge builds cooperation and collaboration. Relationships are key to leadership.

Malala Yousafzai, shown here, is a world-renowned activist and leader in the struggle for social justice for all. She works tirelessly to spread her message and encourage others.

We Think Twice is a teen leadership platform supported by the U.S. Department of Health and Human Services. Encouraging teens to become change makers, they identify the qualities of effective young leaders as:

- **standing up for what you believe in**
- **respecting others and being fair**
- **seeking opportunities to help others**
- **being a role model**
- **encouraging others to set and achieve goals**
- **following positive role models**

We Think Twice has a song list on Spotify selected by teen leaders for inspiration. What song would you pick?

Chapter Eleven

A TRUE LEADERSHIP STORY

A small number of students showed up at a meeting. A teacher announced the meeting with the goal of creating a safer, more respectful, and more caring school. A violent event was the tipping point after conflict, intolerance, prejudice, and negative attitudes affected many students in the school. Problem solving was their goal.

This small group set goals and experimented with creative solutions. Some strategies worked. The students found allies by communicating with other clubs and service organizations in the school. The group got bigger, and more students knew about their efforts. Communication of their message and values turned up everywhere. They held meetings that were open circles of discussion and sharing of hopes and ideas, successes, and next steps. Teams took on projects, and their natural talents helped determine roles and responsibilities. No leaders were elected. The club chose leaders by recognizing the most devoted and hardworking students. Leaders grew in confidence and dedication.

This group kept growing. They designed a T-shirt logo, wrote a mission statement, and painted it 10 feet tall at the entrance to the school. They launched huge communication efforts and drew many students to their programs and events. They became allies with community groups that matched their mission. Other local schools started similar clubs. Their efforts led to a yearly celebration of creativity and caring. They changed their school for the better. The club recently celebrated its 25th year of action for a respectful school community.

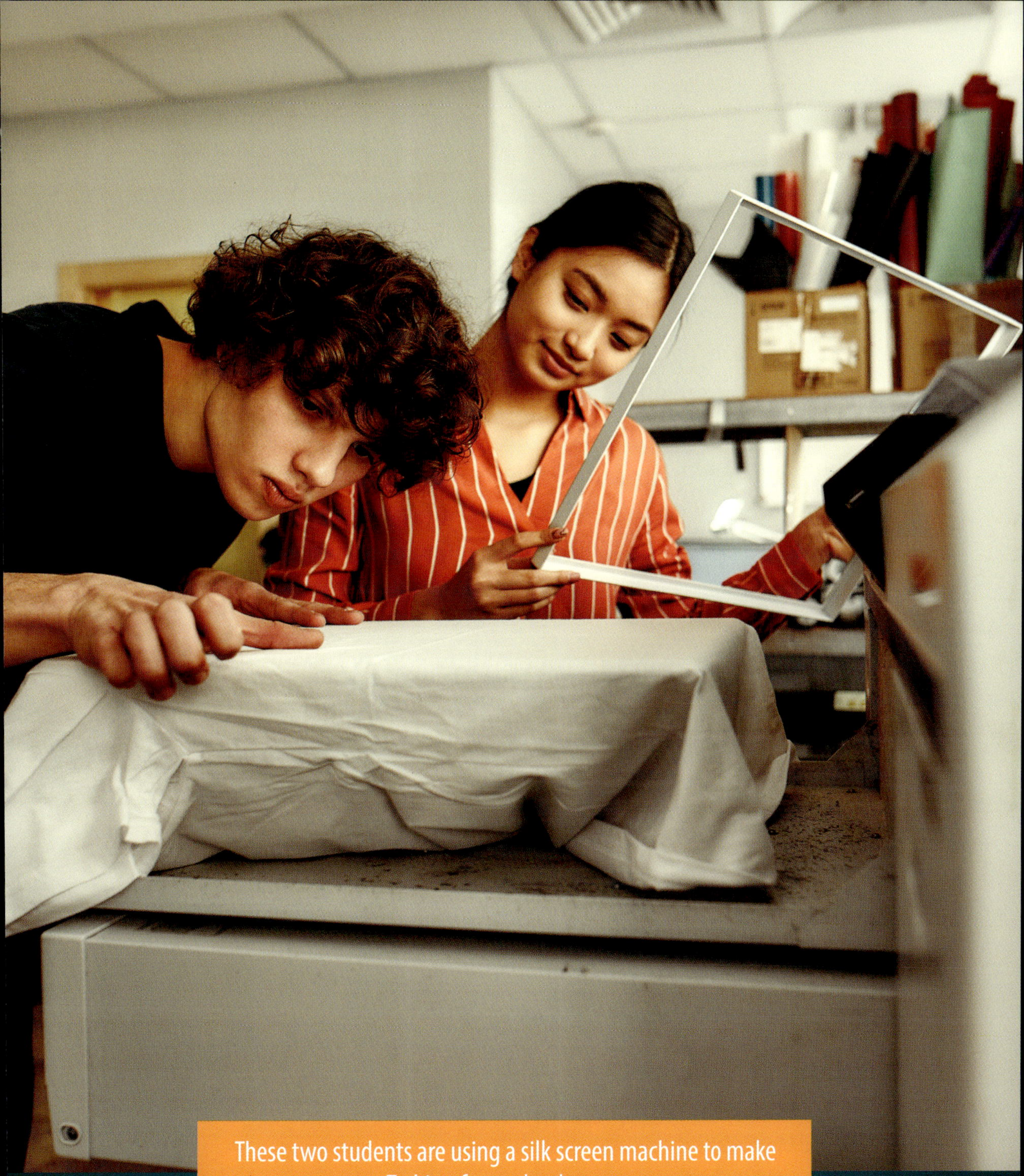

These two students are using a silk screen machine to make T-shirts for a school event.

Chapter Twelve

SOLUTIONS

It is possible for everyone to learn about civic participation and actively improve their communities. Educators from your social studies teacher to your principal to national leaders and experts know this. Young people learning how to participate in their community is the key to problems being solved. Learning to be an active citizen is the first step in becoming part of the solutions.

The National Council for Social Studies guides what you learn in middle school and high school. Their efforts have launched a new vision for a high school graduate. Many states have goals for their graduates to be active citizens. Active citizens work to make a difference in their community. They develop knowledge, skills, values, and motivation to be ready to make a difference. Problem solving,

A science teacher discusses the importance of organic food processes and shares her knowledge with the class.

By gathering together and discussing problems in the world, community members can affect change.

decision making, teamwork, and creativity along with learning through experience are the skills needed for civic action. That learning is a solution that changes the role of adolescents in their communities. Using that learning leads to creative solutions for problems that are important to you and your peers.

Progress covered in news stories from around the nation and world highlight social studies in action. Community-based actions show how students take charge to make a difference. Unique activities are shaped by the types of communities these students live in, the issues most pressing to them, and the tools they have to work with at the time. Students, teachers, and school communities connect with their real worlds creating solutions.

Chapter Thirteen

THE MANY FACES OF CREATIVE SOLUTIONS

Creating solutions has an energy all its own. Exploring how this works leads to an exciting realization—creative solutions happen everywhere around you. Solutions are expressed in art, music, science, services, generosity, caring, and so much more.

Like many other cities, Philadelphia, Pennsylvania, has areas with rundown houses and business. Graffiti covers many buildings. The state of these communities meant many people didn't want to visit them. In 1984, Philadelphia officials came up with a brilliant solution. People arrested for graffiti were given the choice of jail or work for a mural project. Some 3,800 murals eventually transformed the city. Three-story murals with inspiring color, size, beauty, and meaning changed the character of the streets. Philadelphia now creates an amazing and lively response to their cityscape by combining running and artistic murals. Tours of the murals for runners combine athletic workouts with insight to the art that brought many to a creative space and a creative place, their community.

Small towns and cities have creatively solved problems experienced by people who are new to the United States. People fleeing war or oppression come to towns like yours. People seeking a better life come with many needs and few resources. Communities have created projects such as All Are Welcome Here to meet the needs of refugees and immigrants. Communities organize English language lessons at local libraries, assistance with housing and food, legal help, emergency assistance, and information access. Flyers in multiple languages and volunteers who speak several languages provide help and goodwill.

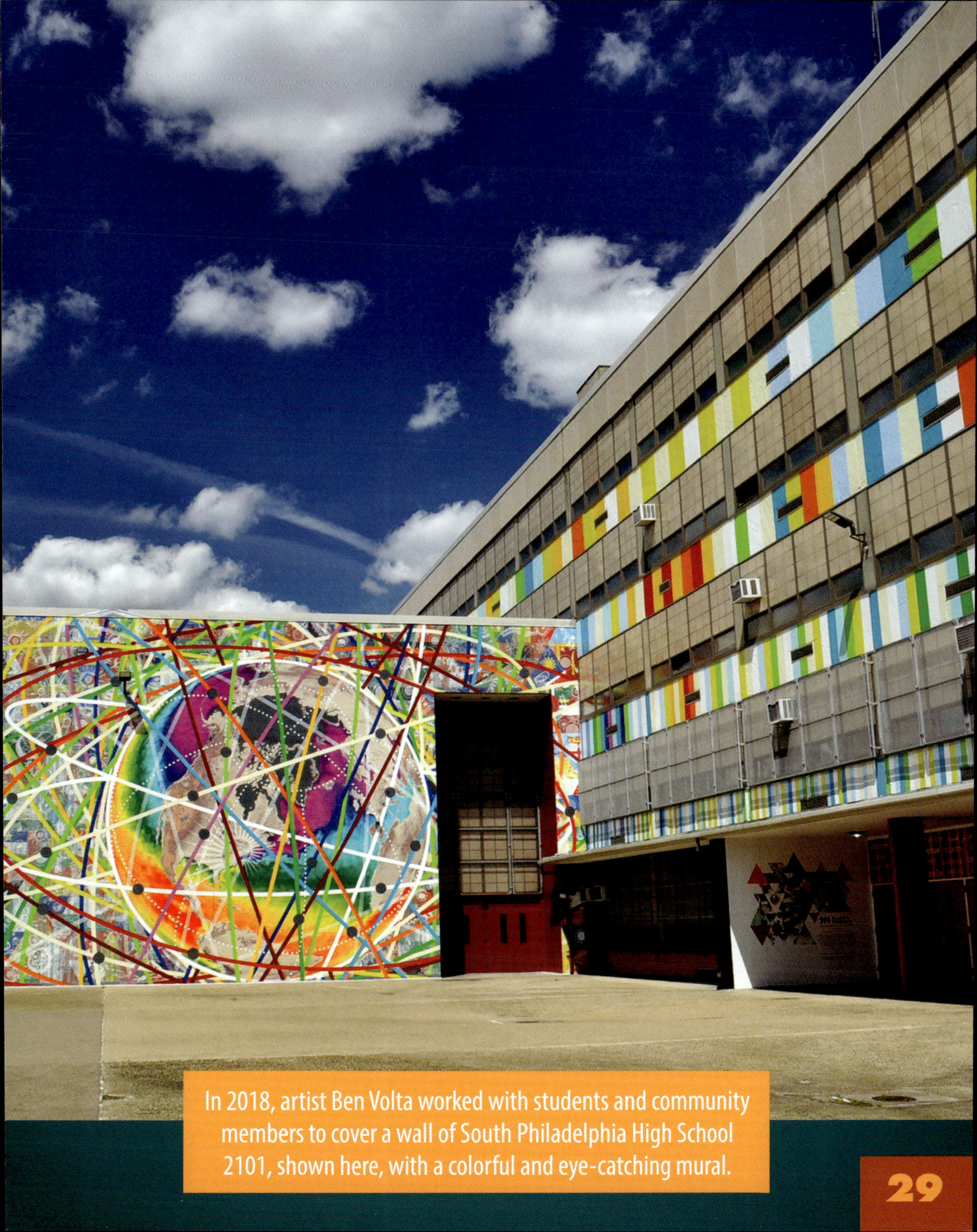

In 2018, artist Ben Volta worked with students and community members to cover a wall of South Philadelphia High School 2101, shown here, with a colorful and eye-catching mural.

Chapter Fourteen

THE DIFFERENCE YOU MAKE

"You cannot get through a single day without having an impact on the world around you. What you do makes a difference, and you have to decide what kind of difference you want to make." This message from wildlife expert Jane Goodall comes from a woman who has made an enduring difference for the planet and its people. She has solved problems for Earth's living creatures. Think about your power to decide what kind of difference you want to make.

Daniel Rivera, an art student at Berlin High School near Albany, New York, won a competition for artists ages 13 to 18 sponsored by the Smithsonian Institute in Washington, D.C. His painting, titled *Tears of Miss Justice: Mourning a Broken System*, draws strong emotions from the viewer. Capturing so much unfairness and the price of injustice, the painting moves minds and hearts to face a hard truth. The painting will be displayed in U.S. embassies around the world.

A young video editor named Sequoia Lowe decided to share the reality of his mother and her experiences with Parkinson's disease. Hardship, pain, and challenges with movement, speech, and mental health with Parkinson's are often misunderstood. His video called *Slim Shaky* won a film competition for the 2023 World Parkinson Congress in Spain. Expressing positive messages, the film features Joni Lowe and her friend with the same disease. *Slim Shaky* now makes a difference in the lives of many people all over the world.

GLOSSARY

advocacy: The act or process of supporting a cause or proposal.

celiac disease: A hereditary intestinal disorder in which an inability to absorb gluten results in an immune response that damages the intestines.

collaboration: Working together for a common goal.

combine: An event at which scouts from the teams in a professional sports league gather to evaluate players before deciding who to draft.

consequence: A result or effect of an action or condition.

critical thinking: The act or applying reason and questioning assumptions in order to solve problems.

empathy: Being aware of and sharing another person's feelings, experiences, and emotions.

ethics: A set of moral principles.

mentor: To teach, give guidance, or give advice to someone, especially a less experienced person. Also, the person who give guidance to a less experienced person.

oppression: Cruel or unjust use of authority or power.

Parkinson's disease: A disease chiefly of later life that tends to get steadily worse and is marked especially by stiff and trembling muscles, slowness of movement, and a shuffling way of walking.

prototype: An original model on which something is patterned.

sensory sensitivity: A condition when someone is particularly bothered by sensory stimulus, such as talking, crowd noise, and busy locations.

truant officer: Someone whose job is to find kids skipping school.

volunteer: Offer to do something for free.

INDEX